FINISHING LINE PRESS

www.finishinglinepress.com

Not pictured

poems by

Kimberly Wright

Finishing Line Press
Georgetown, Kentucky

Not pictured

ACKNOWLEDGMENTS

Thanks to all who helped the development of the works in this book
and my development as a poet, including Sue Walker at the University
of South Alabama, valuable conference help from Barbara Hamby and
encouragement in my teens from Elizabeth Irvine, the English teacher who
gave all us outcasts at Shaw High School in Mobile, Ala., a safe space to
express ourselves. Many thanks to Lee Rozelle and Madison P. Jones, who
helped whip this collection into shape over many lunchtimes. Thanks to
Mom, Dad and all who helped light the way. A special hug for my dear son,
Oliver W. Harper, who keeps me centered.

"Leaving" first appeared in *Blood Lotus Journal.*
"The Dog Meditations" first appeared in *Poydras Review.*
"Too forgotten for slogans" first appeared as "Marginalia" in *Southeast
        Review Online.*
"Always So Much War in Love" first appeared in *Eunoia Review.*
"Michael's Midtown Cafe, Mobile" first appeared in *UCity Review.*
"Terrarium," "En El Cielo, Fronteras No Hay," and "On the Origins of
        Chorizo" first appeared in *Dr. Hurley's Snake Oil Cure.*
"Getting there is part of the fun" first appeared in *Into the Void."*
"Your son's birthday party" first appeared in *Panoplyzine.*

Publisher: Leah Maines
Editor: Christen Kincaid
Cover Art: *Untitled* by Oliver William Harper
Author Photo: Darleen Prem
Cover Design: Elizabeth Maines McCleavy

Printed in the USA on acid-free paper.
Order online: www.finishinglinepress.com
                also available on amazon.com

Author inquiries and mail orders:
Finishing Line Press
P. O. Box 1626
Georgetown, Kentucky 40324
U. S. A.

Table of Contents

For Mom and Oliver

I

The condoms we'll use on Mars

Hope there's a lovely Earth out tonight, you whisper,
voice crackling like aluminum foil
taunting sweet nothings via satellite
as I, sheathed in my encounter suit,
squint toward a diminished sun
watching a sundown melting into the orange hereafter
unobstructed by skyscrapers we've planned, everything
embryonic and distant, like holding hands
while wearing oven mitts, your smile
encased in polymers that allow us to exist
as intruders stumbling over endless red rock hills
and intent. In a makeshift module of wires, tubes,
metal, oxygen and freeze-dried meals, we'll go over the schematics
via comm link, seed little outposts bubbling like a clutch of frog's eggs,
in West Utopia's plains, white picket fences knitted in a blimp
of recycled air, streets, cul de sacs and a corner pharmacy on a someday
stretch of what is now just striated rock, where I will avoid eye contact
with the cashier, brazen prophylactics on the counter,
the thinnest yet invented but more durable than sheepskin,
more convenient and satisfying than latex named after men of war,
made for her, for her pleasure, but it's always the same,
the instructions on tiny paper folded in eighths
so small you'll blink and lose it
studying ink blotches while perched on the toilet,
trying to match the diagram to the living specimen,
drawing on physics to triangulate insertion, concerned gravity
will cause it to slide out, break apart in re-entry,
or an allergic reaction to the mesh will scuttle
every other sensation except itch. And how much
does it cost to ship the damn things from Earth?
And how can I extrapolate the need for such
in nonexistent air charged by distant suns?

Saturn

Stars don't align properly.
Been smelling the turpentine

of failure on this one for a while, white body
a cold planet bloated with methane,

slunk out in the middle of the night,
claimed he couldn't go back to sleep.

I had glided out of his orbit,
playing possum

on the couch when he departed
without a word, the noise betraying—

big bang of the storm door crashing against him
as he dropped something in the doorway.

I imagined his eccentric wobbles
in the front yard's dark

stumbling over the Milky Way's chipmunk holes
and asteroids, the rocky matter

of Saturn's rings uneven as the fumbling
moves of so-called courtship,

the dance of the sprained ankle,
stars too dim for him to chart a course—

no vision, no *ganas*, no O2 to support breath.
The only Saturn he can locate—

the white one he rode in on.
He who drives a Saturn

has hard time finding parts—
(not the only thing no longer being made.)

When it breaks down like he's broken down,
slam the hood and haul it off.

Queen mattress

Abdicate the urge
to leave the bed half-empty.
Margins must widen.

Hit the space bar
click click click
to move like a typewriter carriage
until the royal butt reaches center.

Torso and legs curl
like a question mark
of doughy half-sleep
in the bed's focal point,
capital city of counted sheep
tan sheets with mauve flowers
jolt like ripples on a lake
into mutated hallucinations.

Sometimes too-warm arms and legs
poke out for horizontal perambulations
into chilled hinterlands.
Marginal areas are soon warmed
and, by royal caprice, vacated again
to let cool
to the base temperature of alone.

Always so much war in love

At honeymoon's dusk, we waited
on the Australian coast for the landfall
of little penguins. Wind screamed in,

Antarctic, your Southern blood congealed
and lo, complaints strafed me
like an artillery barrage

you frowning like a general
whose suffering wasn't well paid.
Instead of a penguin invasion,

a bloodless, feathery Normandy Beach,
just a handful waddled forth
bleary-eyed and annoyed

at voyeurs. Park security nabbed
a camera-wielding invader
lining up a tight shot behind

penguin lines. That's it. Show's over
like our brief travels together
flaming tanks in the desert

jets jettisoned, sinking in deep
seawater, metal skeletons.
Next stop: barbed wire,
demilitarized zones.

Spider(s), mate or not

I.

A house spider, silver-dollar wide
turned up in my kitchen, almost turning
into a doormat for my shouting son,
but rather than deal death, I rescued

via cardboard and a small plastic bowl,
put bowl over spider, then slid
cardboard under bowl,
bit by bit, trying not to get bitten,

until stymied arachnid skittered,
probing for weakness with tickling legs
and mandibles and from the doorway
screaming I hurled bowl, cardboard, and spider

out. At the same spot the next night,
it reappeared, wicked long-legged
unrepentant. Capture and release again,
this time walking further into the rain cold dark yard,
screaming and flinging. I later railed against the ballsy
two-timer on the phone to my mother,
and we flattened it into a Rorschach test
as mate-happy Mom giggled that the second appearance

was mate of the first spider, seeking her wayward husband,
while solitary I gleaned one repeat visitor,
the mirror-same spindly tendrils taunting
any idea of mate away.

II.

Mating, for many spider species,
is alpha and omega, female devouring
male during or after, or he, to survive,
detaches from twin phalli

still pumping inside the mate
as emasculated he, if he survives, boasts
a stamina advantage over the double-peckered.
Other species lance the female's abdomen, maiming

to ensure seed speeds to the target,
such deviance reviled by science writers
too wrapped in their skin to see
husks of human predation
drifting like tumbleweed.

Selling it to the fly

Time is food, hungry for more,

I launch, spin, hustle,
my wicked legs, high-wire acrobatics

weaving together fragments,
netted sections of sky wired
porch-post to porch-post

this vision of normal can be yours
the joy of living well—spectacular views!

Oh ne'erdowells, oh legion of flight
all buzzing and fussing about—
how good the gossamer, how sensible it is
to fall into—knitted snug around you

tangled thread, taut, thrums with your struggles

Hold still and wait. This will end well.

Ink pit

When you meet the nonlove of your life
at a toxic waste dump, you don't notice
random guy mired with newsprint,
dust, strangers' sweat.
The coffee cup holds warm muck.

When you meet your future ex at an ink pit,
reality nests like a matryoshka doll,
except what lies hidden
instead of smaller dolls could be gris-gris,
chicken bones, black mold or printing byproducts
dumped decades ago, out of sight, out of mind.

Appearances knit together in walls
and brick, sewer and road, tick and tock,
cyan magenta yellow black in balance
for color photos, only a slight smudge
ink by the gallon, towering reams
of paper. Mammoth presses with metal teeth
devour stray arms of print shop workers,
jaundiced, unblinking graphite ghosts of eyes
haunt newsprint's aging pages.

When you meet a balding Beelzebubba
at a crime scene, you miss the wanted poster
someone forgot to print. The warning
black and yellow of fallout shelter signs
should've read "Stay away" to compensate
for the lack of smoke.

Benzene in lackadaisical drops
seeped in deep, the color of humus-rich earth
bitter like day-old newsroom coffee, carried
in the rainwater, secreted into the sewer,
languishing in groundwater veins,
not suitable to inhale or drink.
Words, smiles, bouquets
shrink to brittle fiber.

When it ends

Initials framed by a heart,
the equation of love
graffiti carved on a tree.

When it ends, hard to erase
without further skinning the bark
Scars linger after you've almost forgotten

what the letters represent. Cutting the tree down,
extracting the stump leaves a hole
where the root system infiltrated,

a crater over which to stumble.

Cellophane-wrapped

Weighed and labeled
priced for quick sale

bloody, marbled mosaic,
alien-looking
liver-colored among rows
of packaged meats
ox tongue, chicken gonads
cattle eyeballs

piecemeal dead spare parts
equal nothing

it once ebbed on
in darkness
bread and water
solitary confinement
catacombs

scratching out
gray days
on reinforced concrete block

twin mattress without sheets
second by second
beat by beat
in institutional cold
no songs except its own
echoing cacophony

anemone arms flailing

no wonder it had to be dealt with
strapped into the gurney

Terrarium

Young men catch snakes for their own good,
rescue what slithered in wide circuit
through ragweed and muck,
retained in glass eight-by-four cubed
with a centimeter-deep pond.
Coiled coffin kings, sterile as pharaoh carapaces,
swallow lab mice dropped in *deus ex machina*, lethargic
without adrenaline spice and palpitating heart.
A sunset of rose hips and orange petals,
lemon custard with meringue clouds
—all this is sealed out.
Tea leaves float in a cooling cup.

Every so often a patch
of gold creeps its way between shutters,
taunts this underworld
of shoe leather, plastic bags,
and Pine-Sol, pungent, stinging a flagellating tongue.
Slave of retreating sun, the liquid gold
slithers away, fading in degrees,
until only a warm spot
remains on the floor.

Color this diminutive mouse life
egg-shell white.
An overhead bulb glows
with the brightness
of a thousand maggots.

Death side of the screen

Little frog skeleton dries
on my mom's screened-in porch
next to the screen, its last moments of starvation
spent within sight of froggy salvation,
a backyard bustling with gnats flying free

while stuck on the death side of the screen
with the patio furniture, houseplants, scoundrel cats
just looking through the screen,

the obvious route denied, sight tantalized so
the creature couldn't look away
long enough to find another way out,
perhaps the amphibian thought an opening
would suddenly appear

allow it to spring forward
into the backyard bounty. Now through patience, it is a perfect
set of bones displayed, bleached framework
of a museum dinosaur in miniature

another folly on its haunches
being rearranged into something
less froglike by the day, once fly-tracking eyes
now tiny white bubbles of pus,

worn-away hull of a tiny shipwreck,
patches of skin a ragged banner on the breeze.

If at first you don't succeed

Experts say you cannot achieve success
without a plethora of failures as immense
as the largest graveyard, a seashore full of sand.
Test the waters for the epic fail, failure to launch,
wardrobe malfunction, stepping on toes,
premature ejaculation, mission abort.
If at first you don't succeed, etc.

Sources close to the matter tell us
doing the same thing over
and expecting a different result
is insanity. Find new ways to fail
to increase your chances of succeeding
or just to vary the types of failing you do
for the amusement of your family and friends.
Variety is the spice of life.

Read a variety of self-help books,
eight-paragraph articles on the web,
a list of tips numbered to solve
every problem you have, even some
you don't. On your bathroom mirror, stick
inspirational quotes on multicolored sticky notes—
be the words you see, take 30 minutes a day
to exercise, an hour for a hobby, grow food,
churn butter, make homemade tortillas, dozens
of sepia full moons, volunteer at your child's school,
another parent lost in the dried macaroni margins,
fit 35 hours of a day into 24 and somehow
find ways to get 100 percent of your daily
allowances of every vitamin and mineral,
eight hours of sleep and eight glasses of water.

If the self-help books and brain doctors have taught us anything,
love, it's that relationships are built on four pillars,
like leg tables, and ours doesn't have a leg to stand on.

Let's call it a night, better to have loved and lost, etc.

Check engine

Constant as the North Star
in the dashboard constellation

an ignored warning on the black and orange horizon
where glowing indicators and digital numbers
twinkle, silent and constant, from the metal, plastic, circuitry

occasional grunts and groans mixed in from the beyond
among the grumbles of the living engine, struggling
like we all do over the hill, the burden of gravity

wheels rattling over the same pitted pavement
between here and there, star stuff the dust on the hood,
a cosmos of a thousand small paint scratches

and in the cabin the odometer spirals,
getting closer to the end as the numbers grow,
bad news deferred until the go is gone.

Michael's Midtown Cafe, Mobile, AL

Preteen school nights sometimes found me
in a store room as wide as I was tall
half-forgotten among boxes, restaurant clatter
and chatter seeping in at my makeshift desk, where
I wrote marine biology answers while shark en papel,

oysters Rockefeller, caesar salad with anchovy airs,
creme brulee, Rolling Rock streamed
out of the kitchen and disappeared,
returning as oil-blotted paper on heavy white plates,
middens of vacant shells shipwrecked on beds of rock salt
little tubs with singed brown sugar barnacles,

emerald messages in bottles sealed with smeared lipstick kisses
as Jim Morrison crooned *Don't you love her madly,*
and Mom wrenched White Zin bottles open with a pop,
adrift in restaurant smell, so many food aromas congealed,

swimming andouille grease, dirt, crumbs, madness,
baked by the hot steam of the dishwasher,
linen and institutional cleaner, I brought it
home with me, it hitchhiked on my clothes

infiltrated my DNA so that a random Doors
song on the radio unlocks the code, reanimates it
bubbling on the current of memory, iridescent jellyfish
glowing in the murk of 20 years later, long after
that repurposed gas station and I
regenerated again.

Leaving

Leave this campground as you found it, more or less,
though hard to do after nearly a decade. Acres of pine trees chipped and pressed
into mountains of court-mandated legalese—one copy for me, one copy for you.
An uneven moonscape, stumps jut like nubs of rotten teeth.

It takes skill not to trip over dozens of earthen mounds,
all of our burials. Something canine or feline growls,
leaves clawed prints and a maimed teddy bear
bleeding tan stuffing from ripped seams. In-laws smear dust
on family portraits, tell ghost stories in the dark,
cast menacing shadows on the tent.

Clothes I'll never again wear—sequined formal gowns
flowing maternities, boxy business suits of gray and black,
faux animal skins mother never stopped buying for me—I throw into the campfire.
It's warm.

II

An idea of birth

October 29, 11 p.m.—Future mom and dad are asleep.
October 30, midnight—Future mom and dad are still asleep.
October 30, 6 a.m.—He is born.
And from then on, it's the story of my life, he said
of his presumed peaceful, on-schedule delivery-as-package
and I wish he could have written his own script,

no days of labor without end, no bossy nurses
probing latex-covered fingers up places
to "find out where we're at," telling me to breathe,
push, pumping in a drug
to lower my blood pressure, another
to raise it again, no maladjusted IV
swelling my hand the size of Mickey Mouse's,
no numb, shaking in a cold room
of stainless steel everything, staying still
on my side for the needle between my vertebra,
for faceless surgeon plowing a bikini line demarcation
through dermis extracting a little frowning him. But I want to keep

that first cry, reddened face, gourd cranium, tiny arms and legs
unfolding like a tripod, and my first sight of him,
ideas ripening in his mahogany eyes.

Your son's birthday party

A yellow amoeba you can pretend
is Big Bird melts across the ice cream cake,
your son too young to recognize
how unrecognizable the bird is,
but your case of the ho*use isn't ready yet* jitters
hits right before the swarm is expected to descend

in various themes of wrapping paper, enormous gift bags,
envelopes full of well-wishes and money.
Must ready the bags of plastic Made in China parting gifts
for kids who won't show, all except your child's cousins
from his father's side and a pair of ex-co-worker's sons
twitching spasmatics loud as a whole room of kids,
who will reduce into pictures in an album and who will not
be absorbed into your child's small circle of friends—
they are older, your child will go to a different school.
In-laws line the walls of the living room.
Granddaddy laces his thumbs through his belt loops,
ponders what teams the boy will follow,
foreseeing a long list of invitations he'll have to decline.

In the glare of the kitchen light, your future ex-husband
tries to warm the knife enough to cut
the solid ice cream block. It gets stuck.

Not pictured

In the first-grade hall, among colorful
stick-figure depictions of weekends
at the beach, wavy blue lines of oceans
and distorted m's of birds in flight,
my son created a crude family portrait,
a cozy brown roof over him
and his dad, smiling stick figures
labeled with large arrows Me, Dad,
and the explanation:

I wish I could be with my dad whenever I want.
This picture is what I'm talking about.

and me, mom of the nuclear family nuked
not pictured but here anyway, bare
under unkind fluorescents, my home's walls
invisible, hand-me-down furniture.
If art imitated life, my stick-figure face
would be tomato red, back knife-wounded.

Come fever and nightmare time
at oh-my-God dark a.m., I emerge,
unphotogenic in a tattered sleepshirt
tousled hair delirium and corner
of mouth crust, changing vomit-soaked bedsheets
and checking temperature. Please
don't show anybody that.

What's going to happen to us?

Uh oh, what happened to our car?
age 4, you addressed the matter
of the white-crusted auto after a rare snow.

What is going to happen to us?
you piped up as we walked
onto a pier to view Fourth of July fireworks,
you stiff like a dried starfish before I took your hand,
told you we'd be safe, and you stepped out,
water lapping below, glint of electric light
swirling on the crazed surface.

What would happen if it was 200 degrees outside?
You thumbed through pages I wanted to hide a little longer,
asked about Lincoln and Lennon's assassinations
Heaven's location on the star chart, monitor
shades of burnt on the drought map.

The U.S. had enough and put bombs on Japan,
you wrote in a report about Sept. 11
as if to say in questions of war,
insert random nation here.

The seas are rising. People will drown,
you said as you dipped into meltwaters
of shrinking glaciers and ice caps, but I blotted
you dry and fudged the facts, said it is not as fast
as a cartoon faucet on full-blast,
water reaching the ceiling until the door
bursts, no, people have time
to react, and already are.

Where does gasoline come from?
you asked on a long ride home,
and when I said we distill
from the extinct, you drilled
into the strata to uncover

how will we get places
when the last dinosaurs propel
out tailpipes. Smart people are creating
electric cars, will fix everything, I claimed,
as we're driving nowhere good, fast,
words melting like Southern snow.

At the Prado with my six-year-old

A Biblical house of horrors,
Christ and the martyrs suffer and bleed
exquisite dark oils folded in the saint's scowls

figures rendered with fiendish rigor, nestled
among cherubs and landscapes, bloodletting
and pale Jesus in death faint, halls where my son floated

cherubic from endless room to room, hall to hall
section to section, with me in a dazing maze
two of thousands lost looking for culture

until he gasped, asked why we need blood—
I keep seeing it, and I can't stop thinking about it!
hid his eyes, surprising me, finding myself

keratinous among medieval torture
bony fingers of what fury belief blossoms into
bleeding Christs whipped in the streets

set on fire, broken over the wheels
or calcifying alongside IV machines
warriors swarming into a sea of knives

broken, bleeding rags drifting
across battlefields—wind's playthings.

Thursday

One droopy drunken eye
taillight, silver Buick
tired twilight

boy in the backseat
communing with a comic book
a blaring headlight
from the back window
illuminates technicolor tales

Front row

Easy to spot, he heads the class, out in front
grouped with whomever chance ordained he spent
the year with, numbered school days of hellos and goodbyes

fill-in-the-blank girls with freckles and reddish hair
dot-to-dot fleshy, Miracle Gro boys take up
more space than he. No matter, it's easy to see

energy in his smile's various wattages,
year after year flashing awkward grins
on the command of "cheese," standing still,

trying not to blink when the light hits
despite the winking of brightness, lamp heat
on the front row, singled out for placement

he wouldn't himself choose, shortest in front
some trick of genetics, tiny ribbons of matter
complicated schematics, symbols we can't read

develops us into us, at least partially
a typical shot, classmates' disembodied heads
loom, grinning gargoyle guys in the background

compact or gangly, bony brittle or Stay-puft soft
around the burgeoning matter of us, just frames
that photographers and morticians are paid to arrange

Packed lunch

Busy day, we ran out of time
to pack tomorrow's lunch together

so I press grape tomatoes, plucking the firmest
for your salad with black olives,

no dressing, pack crackers, apple,
put non-perishables in dented metal lunchbox

thinner, smaller than ones I remember as a kid,
fill a somewhat telescoped reusable water bottle

another of the satellites of bottles rattling
my cabinets, one no longer twists shut

must stay upright or it will leak, I work
to vary the menu but even so

sometimes by lunchtime you find
the meal plan unappetizing

and you return home empty, a paradise
of food hidden away, decaying

Swimming lessons

Q-tip-shaped
giant head, twiggy limbs
test turgidity

of the Y pool
relax, submit
to buoyancy, stretch

like sunbeams
breaking through
cloud's belly into blue

agitated
inhale, coil,
you cling to lifeguard

body curled
into a question
mark, a fear

you can drown in, you know
water kills
just by being water,

but be wise, son, stroke,
kick, think of swimming
as an alliance

exhale danger
as lifeguard asks
you to leap

into the deep
splash
and be plucked

sputtering, enough
to reach
the steps and up

Tasks and lessons

I'm converted to a pixel thing roaming the screen
following directions from an 8-year-old boy coach
Shoot the rocks to get the bonus,
easier said than done, the Wii finger cursor
undulates with the vibration of my nerves.

On a Easter egg hunt, in addition to candy in pastel eggshells,
in a large eggshell with air holes he carried home
scores of roly-polies, pills of reluctant pets he and his friends collected.
Internet search revealed the creatures savor fruits and veggies sliced up,
as well as water in small plastic lids, refilled careful drop by dropper drop
so not to drown the mommy and daddy and baby roly polies,
whole proper families, thriving communities he was convinced
developed on the car ride home. Just like that.

These tasks conscripted
like rescuing earthworms with bare fingers after a deluge.
Following my inclinations, I'd be inside looking out
or finding some more mundane usefulness,
paying bills instead of tweezing between squeamish fingertips
the squirming living pasta, invertibrate flesh
oncoming sun would otherwise sizzle
dried French onion brown almost indistinguishable as worm
but here in the terrarium, he says, here
we'll keep them safe, wet, give them dirt to eat,
release them into a subtropical garden later
before going out of town, the lesson of worms learned.

Quail call

Momma, that was a quail.

If you say so, son.

Among mumbles, muffler rumbles,
cricket chirps, he discerned a warble
I couldn't tell from any generic bird
squawk, cluck, hoot, cardinal trills
and guttural caws of crows,
forms and sounds I misinterpret

among severe-visaged,
beaked, feathered, unsmiling
inmates of Edgar Allan Poe's
nightmares, baked in a nursery rhyme pie
or swooped in Hitchcock menace,
talons carving flesh, bloody hieroglyphs
in black and white. He doesn't know

those birds. His sly ear developed
a well-feathered kinship knit even before
he could pronounce the word bird—
ba-um in toddler tongue—saw them
from below with chubby-cheeked awe
and captured flocks on paper,
bounding seas of crayon ems,
a two-dimensional cage his cognition escaped,
yet he has not lost that soaring feeling
while I strain to pick a warbling treble
out of the white noise.

Wiffle ball

Plastic white egg hatches
endless backyard innings
as mother and son take turns
swinging for fences
that we don't have, missing
the mythical strike zone
over a pine straw home plate

stings a bit to catch and be hit
by this mosquito nip, not anything
like the heft of real baseball, no worries
about broken bones or windows.

My son runs every base,
exultant, crestfallen, silly,
complaining about the fairness
of called balls and strikes.
Sometimes his attitude stinks
more than a jock strap dripping wet
with a summer game's worth of sweat.
He tries on his father's grating whine,
nose wrinkled, the faint of a sulk,
a case of the vapors, little arms
poking through gaping armholes
of a man's baseball jersey.

II.

Playing wiffle ball with his father a decade ago,
I stood smirking on an imaginary pitcher's mound
and threatened to bean him, only to discover
some men like when you hold life in your hand,
bizarre, the power of pain as aphrodisiac.
With an off-target remark, I struck a mark
I hadn't been aiming for and landed a son

saddled with odd bits of his parents,
an inability to see things in plain sight
even when given specific direction,
the way he holds his breath while concentrating
like his constrained father,
squeezing out air every 30 seconds or so
in a constipated straining.

III.

Sometimes I want to forfeit the game,
send him to the shower,
unwind his genetic code, pick out
tawdry hand-me-downs, display them at a yard sale
in a shoebox alongside baseball cards of catchers
too hobbled for Hall of Fame,
or leave at a thrift shop, gossamer strands of being
exuding cardboard-flavored bubblegum.
as middle-aged ladies squinting through bifocals
hold them up, looking for a bargain.

Little guy bounds over the turf,
oblivious to all but play,
reaching behind a bush
with little thorns on each leaf
for a ball that ricocheted.
Guaranteed pain, he will complain
and torque the ball hard,
hole-ridden plastic whirring like a cicada,

hours tallied by pencil
in hand-drawn scoreboard boxes.
Dust clouds of laughter rise up
after each race to the first base tree,
close call, tag out, the magic
of hurtling to nowhere special.

The little weatherman

You examine the figures like a grandfather, brows furrowed
like the Alabama fields of your farmer ancestors
as you share data about the exact expected minute of sunrise and sunset
the percentage of water vapor in the air, the amount of ultraviolet radiation
hitting our provincial skins, the chance of rain later tonight,
all of your meteorology in sonorous tones, relishing the details
you assess line by line, a parade of birds
on telephone wires with leadfeet drivers
careening below. You point them out
during the drive to school, write imaginary tickets
as high clouds drift like smoke over the rich earth
of your brown eyes, obscuring daylight. You think
they're arguing with the sun.

I hope the sun wins, you say.
I hope you win, my son.

III

The dog meditations

I.

Exhalation of doglike warm sea air
with hints of what's rotting in you, wrapped
in fur laziness with doggy smell and teeth,
destroyer of worlds and work,
best friend and worst enemy.

II.

Pain comes in on puppy paws,
carried in the cage of scimitar claws,
snarling, eye-twitch, Let slip the dogs of war?
Loving lick on cheek
or canines crunching carotid?
How does human taste,
mahogany, hints of iron-rich vermilion
distilled echoes of asparagus,
bouquets of perspiration, a sprinkling
of aluminum, tubed on, mass-produced?

III.

Clasped in dog's white teeth, the fledgling
a ball of moist feathers, saliva-wet warm muck,
pink flesh like plucked chicken in cellophane
limp like canned asparagus

IV.

Light brown hairs of dog shed
innumerable like evening stars
twinkling on the indigo of my shirt

hair of the dog that bit me must taste
just like the hair of the dog that licked me.

V.

Dogged, on haunches,
stretching updog and downdog
determined to have its day,
sleep on the floor and wake up with fleas,
whimpering, scratching out madness
bringing the dog to heel, or to hell.

VI.

The dog days of summer, dazed
heat a heavy blanket of panting fur,
gnats hum and swirl, satellites
of aqueous humor, too fast
and flimsy to swat

VII.

Stuck under dog, lap claimed
body concrete-sack heavy but warm,
let sleeping dogs lie or face growling.

The monster

Sometimes there's a monster under your bed
all teeth and claws, and you make believe
it's just shadows, tumbleweeds of dust, stray socks.
There's a burglar at the window, scratching
at the frame, not a wooden finger disturbed
by wind. Snakes, all poisonous, hunger
for an ankle. Spiders, all black widows,
lie in wait in your socks, and you're miles
away from a cure. The man in the black cape,
decked out in formal wear and slicked-back hair,
is really a vampire, prowl by night,
sleep by day, draining you white.

Sometimes it's not only a test of the emergency broadcasting system
as fury of winds, waves and armies knock down your door,
funnel cloud, car, tank, missile barreling toward you
in a totalitarian, tombstone gray mass, and stupefied
you can't or won't move your concrete feet
an inch. The bomb explodes, concussion wave
knocking you end over end. Sometimes you become

shattered glass embedded in your scalp, a tattoo
of numbers etched on your forearm, a family album
filled with ghosts, an unraveled spool of yarn
tangled for miles and decades.

Jobber

You can tell the jobber by the uninspired entry music
and every-other-guy trunks—either solid-color briefs
or old-school Greco-Roman straps
below a slightly out of shape gut or nonsteroidal abs
circa 1980s Mid-South Wrestling
with blonde mullet and dime-store grin. In the audience,
you see no signs asking for his hand in marriage,
no signs calling for him to get suplexed. He walks
to the ring with fake bluster that leaves
no wake, and as the commentators dress him up
as a possible threat to the champ, early on,
he gives his scripted all, ropes the favorite,
lands stunning blows, generates momentum,

but it hits a wall, the called-for shift, one attack countered
and soon it's curtains for the non-contender
sucking up the dust of the mat as the referee taps
thrice. Think of him as the red-shirted guy in Star Trek
except disgraced, not dead, on national TV,
a loss scripted and sure as the maniacal makeup
of the outrageous opponent who, on cue, interrupts
his rival's post-match interview, wiping from memory
what's his name, the defeat a low-calorie filler
leading up to the main bout. We forget
all about ourselves soon enough.

Disposition of the corpse

We made cars in our image,
vessels in which surge a disgusting assortment
of hazardous fluids, high voltage, hoses and wires,
things that must be monitored, flushed, not touched.

Our urine, blood, tears, mucus,
stomach acid, feces, vaginal secretions
give way to oil, gas, hydraulic and transmission fluids,
freon, battery acid. When new,
we are beautiful, state of the art,
a pride and joy heralded in billboards, parties and photo albums
bathed in wax, holy water and baby oil
shrouded with tarps and blankets
primed and sent on our way
with a slap on the bottom, a tap on the gas pedal.

When we collide, go wrong, gush,
explode, sputter steam, turn to mush,
oh the mess, the mess. The stuff coursing in tubes
beneath flesh and metal corrodes carapaces.
Time and elements make us Superfund sites
oozing carcinogenic goo out of the fractures
of ourselves. Dealing with the cleanup
requires strict rules of engagement,
protective gear of rubber and latex,

specifics of disposal not always followed.
Some wind up unlawfully used and discarded,
an 11-year-old girl taken from her apartment
late on a summer's night through an unlocked window,
discovered on Thanksgiving by hunters in a hedgerow,
relic of patchy dried flesh on bones,
a tiny tuft of hair twisting on her scalp.
Even diminished, the girl attended a hearing,
testifying in the only way she could,
as a small skin sample zip-closed
in a plastic bag kept in a cooler

across the table from the grinning defective
dangerous thing that collided into her.

Some land far from justice, no chance
of finding the courtroom as they turn
into swirling factory dust, little shards of glass,
melted lumps of metal, rhododendrons of the road,
in great numbers, murderous clockwork
thousands upon thousands, unidentifiable.

Getting there is part of the fun

Loads of tires shredded down to steel belts,
        the debris field complicates the journey
of those speeding between necessities,
        rubber clods to be maneuvered around.

Bondoed 1965 Dodge, a mottled jester
        putters along a mocking 45 mph
in a 70 mph zone, tailpipe rolling out carbon
        like Frisco Bay fog over the mountains,
minus beauty and plus smokiness
        and you're stuck choking, a chicken
locked in a small metal cage, one
        of the delirious, puffs of petrified feathers
a free blur as the impatient whiz by.

In the road's margins scatters bulky scat—
        once whole things someone had
half-assed strapped to a trailer,
        a Sanford and Son collection,
2 by 4s shattered into thorns
        hubcap UFOs bouncing and rolling,
a loveseat with love knocked out of it,
        a Harley worth thousands until
a sudden loss, 70 to 0 in 10
        clattering seconds
decelerating in awkward somersaults,
        a chrome meteor shower.

Torpor topiary

Gray-colored rooms cool, room temperature
the color of shiny iron metal sometimes
with pink flecked by mostly gray wallpaper
dust-covered faded pink of some
long-ago prom dress, pressed flowers

a surprise, sometimes, to see fish tanks
full of life where they exist,
when waiting places bother with the facsimile
of life bubbling by in flipping iridescent fins to amuse
but too often nowadays there's a screen every three feet
feeding us static, bombastic tinny voice booming
from manufactured mouths, alarm in scrolling words
at the bottom, always urgent, shoehorned into
a box with things we don't have but really should need
and singe the eyeballs with dazzling images

and too-white snapping teeth sinking into us
whereas the room is gray, we uncomfortable
in contortionist chairs, elbows sticky
with someone else's grease, populated
with fidgety children who will not stop
being bored and loud while missing
their favorite color of crayon

rolled under the couch, while we hedge
humanity, keep a safe distance from everyone,
don't stare or attempt to discern
what's hidden behind eyeballs,
flaking skin, shedding hair and oozing orifices
eyes set too close together, too far apart,
marinating in the odor of themselves,
maladies they hope insurance will cover,
as disinfectant battles a cavalcade of sneezes
and we're all there, waiting for whatever
and we'll get it eventually, when it's our turn,
when the woman in technicolor scrubs
calls our names

Living tombstone

A dark-haired angel
stitched on her skin
weeps ink

above initials and dates
four loves gone in five years

crosses, hearts, tears etched
on caramel skin

emblems on her back
embossed by sorrow

hands folded
fingers to heaven
hearts and mouths
choking on ink

grim artistry of needles
and what they unearth

bubbling ink
reaching dermis
obsidian

After surgery

Tissues sewn together
incision points
knit themselves whole again

capillaries feeding
regeneration through
ribbon lines of nourishment

recrafting sundered flesh cell by cell
but it's easy to imagine
things aren't quite what they were

fault lines may give
after unusual pressure, after a huge sneeze
tectonic plates under what seems

solid land—even a small slip
can bring a cataclysm
roads, houses and bodies snapped

after several surgeries, a body becomes
a well-traveled landscape of railroad tracks
and interstates, a patchwork quilt
of crisscrossing seams and fabrics.

Good floors

The black glue that held carpet down
onto wood parquet floors in the hall
and bedrooms won't come up

with a good scraping like the seller promised,
nothing good about scraping or anything else
except the price, the clothesline and it's not a trailer.

The carpet, orange, dust and bug leg-ridden
seventies nightmare obscured good wood parquet
or good until a previous owner glued carpet

good and tight, and prying it off took a few parquet
pieces with it—how good parquet turns bad—
old adhesive sullies, disintegrating into dust,

collecting in corners, in eyesockets, tear ducts,
autopsies, entering the A/C vent, from a fine dust
to flakes the tar of every old road I've ever gone down.

The real estate lady shook her head, suggested
wall-to-wall carpeting I can't afford:
            You'll never get the floor the way you want it

so better keep up appearances,
but I'm not buying it. I rattle my rafters, leak
like dripping faucets down

into tissues and pillows, hang
blouses and old socks on the line
cover it all up with area rugs everywhere.

Too forgotten for slogans

Down the path at the end of Gardenia, cut out
by trespassing feet like mine, I wound
next to a ravine so unmarked and unremarkable
Google Maps couldn't tell me

where I'd been. At the beginning of the trail,
a glimmering graveyard of plastic bottles
blossoming like mushrooms feeding on damp,
aluminum cans too forgotten to hold slogans,
solemn rubber tires like evergreen wreaths
in memory of usefulness and trail-blazing
tossed pell-mell to tumble downhill

to this nonrecycling collection point. Sewer caps
like bellboy hats sessile and half-buried
poke out of red clay scarred with armies of ants,
cut bank sliding into tire ruts intermingled with raccoon prints,
a blanket of calico leaves annoyed into patches
of sullen dirt that grooves itself into
the trenches of sneakers, back yards
and brushy trees, tilting oaks swooning,
undermined by landscape erased sooty drop
by sooty drop, destined to collapse

into a chasm with aquamarine PVC pipe teeth,
tarmac and concrete shanks, a deep yaw
100 feet behind a row of houses,
windows unblinking, dormant.

Coronary doppler

My heart—a greedy fish prowling
an inland sea, a frenzied yaw
opening and closing, detected

via doppler in black and white images
but shooting out blue and red flames
dark, alien flesh tremulous trolling

deep beneath the surface in its sunless murk
glimpsed by the light of imagination
sharp-toothed, dangerous, full

of sinister power, constant
in devouring, indomitable churning
in the briny deep plumbed only by sound

below the strata of bones and Sargasso sea
below the limit of unmanned submarines
under pressure more than three times gravity,

where whale echoes whispers
where fabulous tentacles
can snap galleons in two

Old and eating fear

Sullen when your family doesn't heed
your warnings, take their money out of the bank
and buy silver coins, the patriarch *Goddamnit,*

you know YouTube well enough
to track down vacuum noise that transforms into
the Illuminati speaking through Ariana Grande's songs.
See what she sings when you play it backwards.

Dire predictions for $20.99 plus postage and handling;
you buy the book before the dollar becomes worthless
but never open it.

You want to buy an RV to flee
property tax and coming war, armed with
the pump-action shotgun you covet.

You swear your legs are strong enough to push
gas and brake pedals, though not strong enough
to carry you across your tiny bedroom.

It took three grown women
to maneuver the behemoth
         how unbending you are
back onto the hospital bed.

Three Jesuses and two Marys watch while you sleep.
You abandoned two motorized scooters, one in the hallway
near the front door, covered in dust,

the other out on the back patio, covered with a tarp.
You are the metal frame of an electric sign,
the tubes long since snapped, signage disintegrated,

the something that happens when nothing does,
reservoirs retaining dried-up weeds and dust, skies forgetting
how to generate clouds. A watch falls off your bony wrist.

The coupon is expired. Your general practitioner
waits on the line to be cursed and fired.

Earth-bound astronaut

In February 2007, astronaut Lisa Nowak attacked Air Force officer
Colleen Shipman with pepper spray at a Florida airport parking lot
after driving from Texas, allegedly wearing an adult diaper for the
nonstop trip. Behind the attack was Nowak's jealousy over Shipman's
three-month romance with astronaut William Oefelein, Nowak's
former lover.

Not everyone understands
heavenly bodies, the pull
of your gravity
head-over-heels
physics of my near-earth
orbit, somersaulting
in a maximum absorbency garment

They craft Icarus into art
write odes to the pubescent boy
but he never broke the sound barrier
his crude craft
a trick of glue and feathers
never slipped beyond
the planet's freezing outer layer

at some elevation, ice crystals form

at the speed of this re-entry
purity of flame
melts away all but my steel

you spin away
terrestrial treachery
I could see for thousands of miles

Thrusters fire
on an intercept course
the engineered line of I-10
above the curve of the coast
my foot heavy on the floorboard

through dense forests a technicolor rush
of scrub pine, truck stops and fast food
from Johnson Space Center to Orlando
nonstop

sonic boom of descent into a midnight
heavy with menace, pursuit loaded
with accoutrements: latex gloves, a black wig,
a BB pistol and ammunition,

I scan the horizon
senses palpitating like a spinning quasar,
black holes for eyes
the event horizon of which
the she I hunt cannot escape
luring her in with the cloak of mad tears,
the gascous cloud of pepper spray
I spritzed into her car
ears filled with the static-filled ovations of space
only I can hear

my re-entry glows blue hot
like the most powerful stars
relentless detonations
witnessed for millions of miles

Abode among ruins

Dry scales crack, fracture, slough
where no grass grows, nude earth
far beyond anyone's horizon.
No shadow apes me, no glaring
warmth. My scales shield me.

Sometimes sun breaks
like egg yellow on my tongue
through breach of foliage.
My tongue flickers, transient
like sunlight in underbrush
where mold propagates and tree roots
gnarl cold soil, potpourri humus,
dead pawns of spring on which I coil.

Some of us ask for nothing but existence
retina, DNA, cloves, and hollowed ground.
The sun broils and curdles nuclear out
among shrubbery and scrubgrass, not here
among oak-shadowed tumbleweeds of withered armor.

Weed

Sustained, mining vitamins
from gravel and powdery construction zone dust
roots pushing against rocks and stones
perked by bleary-eyed sunrise
pools of vinegar, fists and thorns
plastic wrap dancing on a breeze
A wiry weary filament
among worms and fruit flies
but here unfurled
like a tattered banner
in the boldness of meager existence   am I

Your childhood

Your childhood is falling apart, abandoned
waterpark time forgot, chutes and ladders
to nowhere, some of it auctioned off,
rusting and consumed, an overgrown
field, the ghoulish, running mascara,
a clown face. Your childhood expelled
in fits and phlegmatic coughs,
bursts forth like a rash across hived skin,
red splotches blooming like tiny wildflowers,
swelling purple like a bruise,
deserted, blood-stained underwear in a ditch,
a small pink anemone, billowing.
Your childhood cold and turgid,
silent, concealed and weighed down
in a black plastic trash bag,
bloated and fetid like your dumpster hometown,
your childhood clammy, the belly of a caught carp,
the scalpel cutting across, stainless steel pins
holding open sectioned skin, what lies
beneath nude for examination. Alcohol,
formaldehyde blends with the aroma
of earthy perfume, a swabbed sample
of your childhood, minuscule abstraction
under a microscope, shimmering dots
in a saline solution, a chemical reaction
under glass and hard light, a mystery
deciphered and chronicled, a lengthy
report on legal-sized paper,

this page intentionally left blank.

En el cielo, fronteras no hay

Silvio sings to me
from across the embargo line,
a specter from Cuba decoded off ribbon.
My body, coral reef white, city
fluorescent light, cold as bathtub porcelain,
soaks in the Straits of Florida.
This lilting song blows breath
into debris, what once ventured
across livid ocean and broke apart
into planks engorged with water,
splintered ribs of a galleon
crusted over with limestone
of sessile sea dead that settled
to the bottom. But there is life.
Brain coral mounds, fan coral maroon
on the apex. Gurgles caress, gentle waves
lap twined mangrove roots
where sleek crustacean children sleep.
My hair swirls, a sea anemone
stretching out stinging fingers.
His voice nibbles on my hip.

World begins/ends

The world begins
  with a forgotten phrase
a rain-soaked nightmare
  bedwetting sheets
near Lake Okeechobee

The world begins as the heavenly hosts
  detonate, screaming
across the empty tomb
  of sky blessed assurances

The world begins
  the high pitch of a whale song
as a creature rises
  from the muck crawls out

In a spattering of blood
  the world begins
gargle of an extended rhythm
  in your spine
hum, whirr and click
  of bones, muscle and skin
kick against the soft sides
  of your basket
on your way downriver

The world begins again as river
  as diaspora
step by step, drop by drop
  seeping
to fountain forth again
  clean and whole
through the aquifer
  naturally occurring minerals

One foot follows another
  the well-worn road

dents into   your shoulders
        column creaks
        with the burden

The world continues
        as a protest song
the rhythm of pickaxes
        against granite
howls of the dying
        retort of the battlefield
roars of big cats
        drowned out by the roars
        of airplane

The world imperils party propaganda
        invades your personal space
shatters the livingroom picture window

There are not enough pharmaceuticals
        to deal with the world
There are not enough pharmaceuticals
        to deal with the side-effects
of the pharmaceuticals you take
        to deal with the world

The world ends
        as you take a number, wait
your turn
        meatloaf and potato salad
utilitarian plastic chairs

The world crumples
        into your naugahyde skin

crunched into pie charts
        campaign slogans
a 30-second video

with autotone accompaniment
of that song you always hated
seeping through the static
of all the department stores

The world cannot fit
on your mobile device
not backwards compatible
not a trending topic or user-friendly
does not meet the magazine's current needs
is on permanent hiatus

The Adobe Flash plugin   of the world
has crashed

Kimberly L. **Wright**'s poetry has appeared in several publications, including *Poydras Review, Eunoia Review, Blood Lotus Journal, UCity Review, October Hill Magazine* and *Southern Review Online.*

She graduated from the University of South Alabama, where she and interned for literary journal Negative Capability and served on the editorial board of a campus literary journal. She briefly attended graduate school at the University of Memphis before getting sidetracked into journalism, working in the press for 20 years, including as a copy editor of a daily newspaper.

Kimberly L. Wright was born in Hollywood, Florida, and raised in Mobile, Alabama. She lives in Woodstock, Georgia, with a teenage son, a dog, and a cat.

This is her first collection of poetry.